THIS BOOK IS ....

THE WORLD'S MOST CUTE/UGLY/OBNOXIOUS/DIVINE/KISSABLE/PATHETIC/CHARMING/SEXY/LEO

YOURS IN DISGUST/LOTS OF LOVE

BEST WISHES ....

P.S. PLEASE TAKE NOTE OF PAGE(S) ....

THE LEO BOOK

A CORGI BOOK 0 552 12320 X

First publication in Great Britain
PRINTING HISTORY
Corgi edition published 1983

Copyright © Ian Heath 1983

Corgi Books are published by Transworld Publishers Ltd.,
Century House, 61-63 Uxbridge Road, Ealing, London W5 5SA

Made and printed in Great Britain by the
Guernsey Press Co. Ltd., Guernsey, Channel Islands.

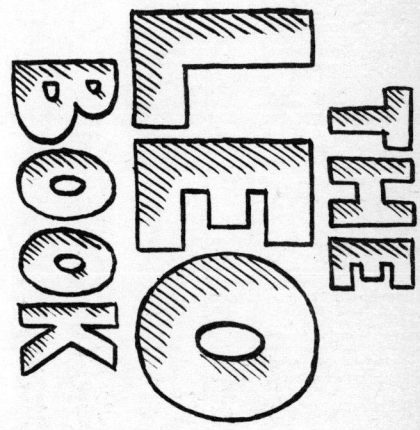

LEO
JULY 21 – AUGUST 21

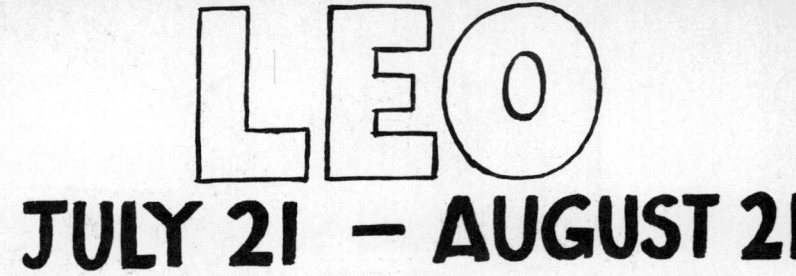

FIFTH SIGN OF THE ZODIAC
SYMBOL : THE LION
RULING PLANET : THE SUN
COLOURS : ORANGE, YELLOW
GEM : DIAMOND
NUMBER : ONE
DAY : SUNDAY
METAL : GOLD
FLOWER : MARIGOLD

...IS INSECURE...

.....HANDLES PEOPLE WELL..........

...IS UNTIDY......

...... WELL-RESPECTED......

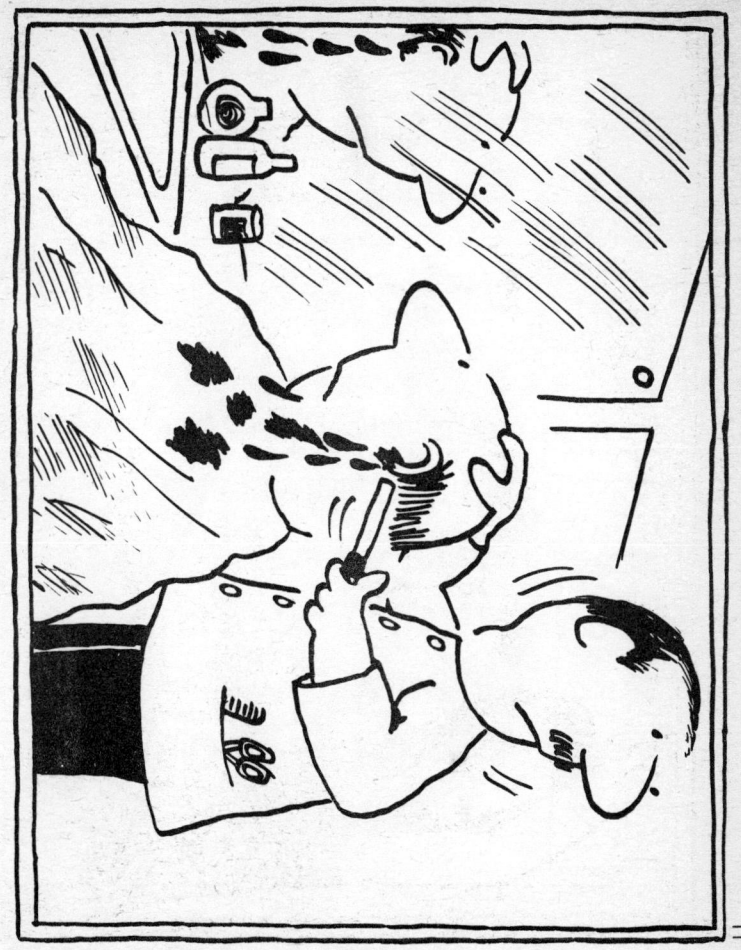

... CAN BE CARELESS ...

... IS NOT VERY TALKATIVE ....

...TAKES RISKS...

.... LOVES APPLAUSE ....

....AND IS ALWAYS RIGHT.

The **LEO** finds success as...

A CARPET SALESPERSON......

...... FINANCIAL WIZARD ....

SCULPTOR..........

.... OSTEOPATH ....

DOG-CLIPPER

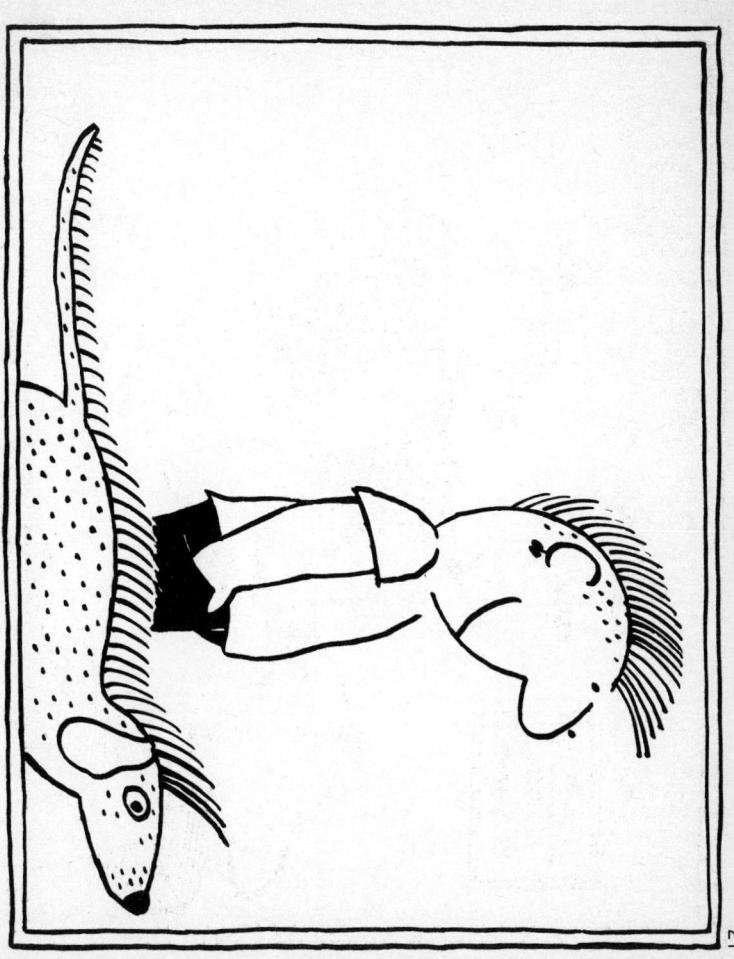

......OR TENNIS COACH.

...IS A DETERMINED GARDENER......

…..KEEPS EVERYTHING SPOTLESS……..

..... DOESN'T LIKE PETS .....

...EATS TO EXCESS..........

......IS A T.V. ADDICT......

...... ENJOYS DECORATING ......

......A SUN-WORSHIPPER..........

..... DOESN'T ANSWER BACK ......

The LEO likes......

......FUNFAIRS......

DOUGHNUTS ....

.... BEE-KEEPING ....

......THE CINEMA......

......TAP-DANCING......

......AND OLIVES.

The LEO dislikes

...BEING TAKEN FOR A RIDE.........

..........DANCING..........

PAYING BILLS..........

...SEAFOOD...

...OTHER PEOPLE'S CHILDREN...

......AND COLD SHOWERS.

The LEO in love

....WHISPERS SWEET NOTHINGS.....

..... FLIRTS A LITTLE .....

...SHOWERS LOVER WITH GIFTS........

....IS AGGGRESSIVE IN BED.........

..... WEARS LOW-CUT DRESSES ......

...NEEDS TO BE ADMIRED......

......IS UNLUCKY......

VERY FIERY . . . .

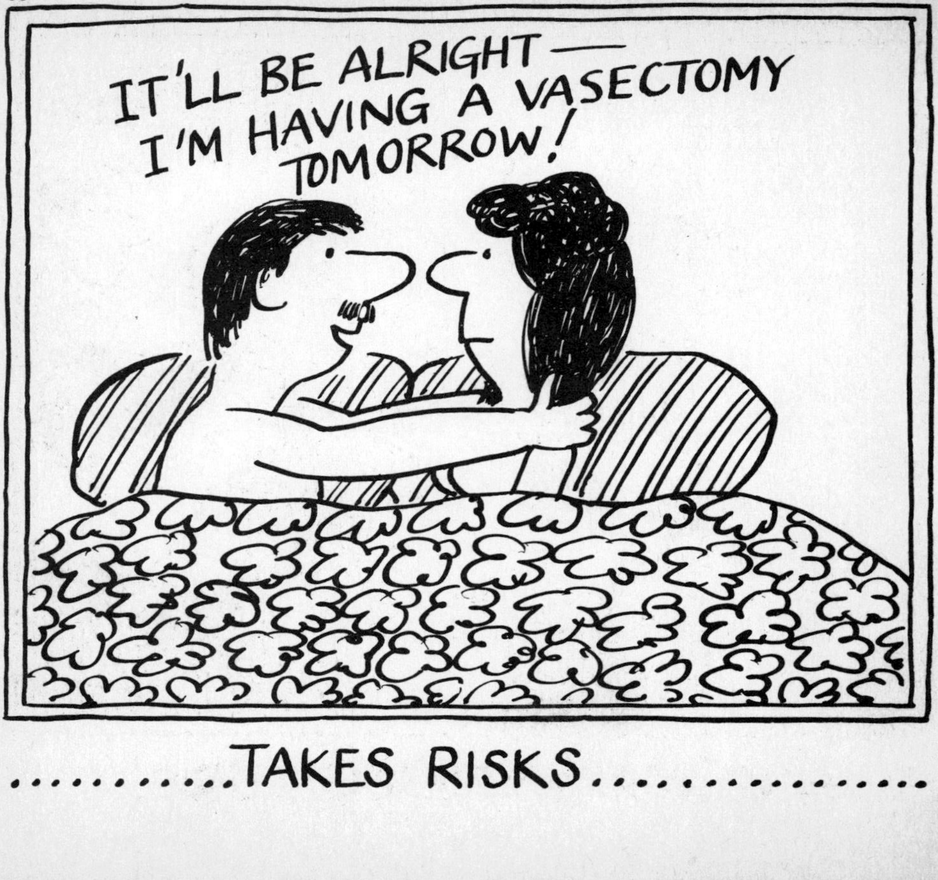

..........TAKES RISKS...............

..... AND MAKES HEADS TURN.

LEO AND PARTNER

HEART RATINGS

♥♥♥♥ WOWEE!!
♥♥♥ GREAT BUT NOT 'IT'
♥♥ O.K. — COULD BE FUN
♥ FORGET IT
♥ WALK QUICKLY THE OTHER WAY

SAGITTARIUS ARIES ♥♥♥♥♥♥
VIRGO LIBRA GEMINI ♥♥♥♥
CANCER
SCORPIO LEO ♥♥♥
AQUARIUS TAURUS ♥♥
PISCES CAPRICORN ♥

LEO PEOPLE

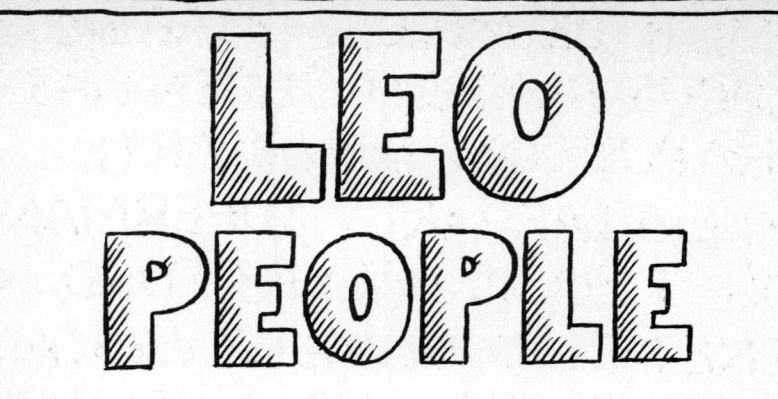

GEORGE BERNARD SHAW
ANDY WARHOL : ROBERT REDFORD
CARL JUNG : ALFRED HITCHCOCK
ROBERT BURNS : ROBERT MITCHUM
NATALIE WOOD : EMILY BRONTË

CECIL B. DE MILLE : MAE WEST
ALDOUS HUXLEY : OGDEN NASH
NAPOLEON BONAPARTE
AMELIA EARHART : SUPERMAN
'COUNT' BASIE : HENRY FORD, SR.
GENE KELLY : ORVILLE WRIGHT
PRINCESS MARGARET : MATA HARI
SHELLEY WINTERS : MUSSOLINI
YVES SAINT-LAURENT : SHELLEY
FIDEL CASTRO : SIR WALTER SCOTT
ROBERT TAYLOR : SAM GOLDWYN